search and
Bible
Stickers 2

With over 50 full-colour, self-adhesive stickers for you to use to complete the pictures.

Su Box and Roger Fereday

Jesus is born!

Mary and Joseph were staying in a stable! There was no room anywhere else – so many people had travelled to Bethlehem to be counted by the Romans.

Far from home, Mary's baby son Jesus was born in that stable. Joseph made Him a bed in a hay-filled manger.

That night shepherds on the hills saw angels in the sky. One angel said, 'Good news! God's own Son has been born in Bethlehem.'

The excited shepherds hurried into Bethlehem. They found Jesus with Mary and Joseph in the stable. It was just as the angel had said. They thanked God for this very special baby – His Son, born to be King.

Wine at the wedding

When He grew up, Jesus did many wonderful things. His first miracle was at a wedding in Cana.

Jesus was at the wedding party with His mother, Mary, and His friends. Lots of other people had been invited and they were all enjoying themselves.

Then there was a problem – the wine ran out.

'Fill those tall jars with water,' Jesus told the servants. Then He told them to give some of the water to the man in charge.

The servants watched as the man tasted his drink. He gave a big smile – the water had been turned into very good wine.

This was Jesus' first miracle.

Jesus calms a storm

Jesus and His friends were sailing across Lake Galilee. It had been a busy day and Jesus was asleep at one end of the boat.

Suddenly a great storm blew up. The wind blew hard and great waves tossed the boat about, splashing water over the sides.

'Wake up!' the frightened friends called to Jesus. 'We're going to sink.'

Jesus stood up. He was not afraid.

'Quiet! Be still!' Jesus said to the wind and the waves.

At once the wind stopped blowing and the sea was calm again.

'Look, even the wind and waves obey Jesus!' said His friends in amazement.

Jesus feeds a crowd

People followed Jesus everywhere to hear what He said and see what He did.

One day, a huge crowd followed Him to the far side of the lake. They listened to Jesus all day and began to feel hungry. Jesus asked His friends to find food for them.

'But there are over 5,000 people here!' said Philip.

Jesus dies on a cross

Many people loved Jesus but He had lots of enemies too. They didn't like what He did or what He said.

They arrested Jesus and asked Him tricky questions. They even took Him to Pilate, the Roman leader in Jerusalem.

Andrew found a boy who had five rolls and two fish to share. Jesus asked God to bless the food. Then He told His friends to share it out.

There was enough for everyone!

No one went hungry and there were twelve baskets of leftovers. It was another miracle!

'Jesus has done nothing wrong,' said Pilate. 'I will let Him go.'
But the people shouted: 'No! Kill Him!'
So Pilate told the soldiers to take Jesus to a hill outside the city. They nailed Him to a cross and left Him to die.
Jesus' friends and enemies watched and waited. At last Jesus cried out, 'My work is finished!' Then He died.

Jesus is alive!

Jesus' friends buried His body in a tomb in a garden. They rolled a heavy stone across the doorway.

At dawn, three days later, Mary Magdalene went to the garden. She saw that the stone had been rolled away and told the other friends.

Peter and John hurried to look. When they found the tomb

was empty, they went away again.

Back in the garden Mary met a man she thought was the gardener.

'Mary,' said the man.

Then Mary knew – it was Jesus! That's why the tomb was empty. He was alive!

Full of joy, Mary ran off to tell her friends the wonderful news.

The amazing catch of fish

Jesus' friends had been fishing all night but their nets were still empty.

Suddenly they heard a man shouting from the shore: 'Throw your nets on the other side of the boat and you will catch plenty!'

The friends did this and at once their nets were full of fish.

Then they knew – the man was Jesus.

'Come and have breakfast,' Jesus called. 'Bring some of those fish to cook too.'

Peter swam for shore and the others followed in the boat. Jesus was already cooking fish over a fire on the beach.

The friends were excited to share another meal with Jesus. He really was alive.

Published 2008 in the UK by CWR, Waverley Abbey House, Waverley lane, Farnham, Surrey GU9 8EP, UK
ISBN: 978-1-85345-478-3

Copyright © 2008 Anno Domini Publishing
1 Churchgates, The Wilderness, Berkhamsted, Herts HP4 2UB England
Text copyright © 2008 Su Box
Illustrations copyright © 1998 Roger Fereday

Editorial Director Annette Reynolds
Editor Nicola Bull
Art Director Gerald Rogers
Pre-production Krystyna Kowalska Hewitt
Production John Laister

All rights reserved. No part of this publication may be reproduced or transmitted in any form or by any means, electronic or mechanical, including photocopying, recording or any information storage and retrieval system, without either prior permission in writing from the publisher or a licence permitting restricted copying.

For a list of CWR's National Distributors visit www.cwr.org.uk/distributors

Printed in China.